Bouboul au Football
Bouboul at the Football

By Opal Dunn
with Marilyn Malin

Illustrated by Annabel Spenceley

CHERRYTREE BOOKS

A Cherrytree Book

Designed and produced by
A S Publishing

First published 1992
by Cherrytree Press Ltd
a subsidiary of
The Chivers Company Ltd
Windsor Bridge Road
Bath, Avon BA2 3AX

Text Copyright © Opal Dunn 1992

Concept development Copyright © Marilyn Malin 1992

Illustrations Copyright © Annabel Spenceley 1992

Language Consultant: Andrew Davis

British Library Cataloguing in Publication Data
Dunn, Opal
  Bouboul au Football: Bouboul at the
  Football. – (Learn-a-Language Storybook Series)
  I. Title II. Series
  448.3

ISBN 0 7451 5164 7 Hardcover
ISBN 0 7451 5183 3 Softcover
ISBN 0 7451 5185 X Softcover & Cassette

Printed and bound in Italy by L.E.G.O. s.p.a., Vicenza

Speaking French

The best way to speak French, with a French accent, is to listen to the cassette and try to imitate it exactly. If you haven't got a cassette, ask someone who knows French to read the French in the book for you.

French people use their lips, tongue, throat and nose in special ways to make French sounds. Some of the sounds may be new to you. So listen to French spoken first and read it later. Notice how different some of the sounds are.

Alphabet letters	The names are different in French. Listen to 'h', 'y' and 'u', for example. There are more sounds in French than there are letters in the alphabet.
Consonant letters – all except a e i o u	These are often silent at the end of words, so you write them but you don't say them. *deux trois*
Letter g	g followed by e or i has a similar sound to the letter j. Otherwise it is hard. *garage sage regarde*
Letter h	h is usually silent *huit heure homme* but is sometimes said from the throat.
Letter j	j is generally soft in French. Say 'jug' in English and then '*je*' and '*jolie*' in French.
Letter r	r is made in the throat, not near the front teeth. Say 'red' in English and then '*rouge*' and '*Murielle*' in French.

Letter e e at the end of words is almost silent, so you hardly notice it *piscine glace* EXCEPT when it has an 'accent aigu' *é fermé* (see below).
ei er ez at the end of a French word is often said like letter *é* with an accent aigu.
est is also said like *é*.

Letter u u has a special sound in French. To get used to saying this sound, say the letter e in English. While saying it, change the shape of your lips from a broad smile to a small hole. Now you are making the sound of the letter u in French.
tu Murielle Mumu

Letter y y by itself has the same sound as the letter i in French. It is like the first sound in the word 'evening'.

Some letters have additional marks that tell you how to say them.

Letter c If there is a little hook below the letter ç (called a cedilla) it shows the sound has changed to an s sound.
ça français

Accents above vowel letters – a e i o u – show a change in the letter sound.

Accent aigu ´   *fermé entrée méchant*

Accent circonflexe ^   *tête plaît côte à côté*

Accent grave `   *là voilà père très*

Contents

Henri was practising for the school match, although he didn't have a proper ball. He and Hervé had already marked the goals when Hélène came up.

'Are you playing?' Henri asked.

'All right,' answered Hélène.

'Play with me,' said Hervé. 'Look. Here, this is my goal.'

Henri pointed across the playground and said,

'And there, that's my goal.'

'All right,' Hélène said again, and Hervé pushed the ball into her hands.

'Take the ball,' he said.

Hélène went to the middle of the playground and they were ready to start.

'Go on, Hélène,' said Henri.

'Wait. One, two, three,' said Hélène, and she kicked off.

'Here, Hélène. Quick,' called Hervé.

Hervé finally got the ball, shouting,
    'It's mine.'
He dribbled towards the goal and then shot.
    'Great, Hervé!' Hélène said.
    'It's a goal,' Henri shouted.

'Come on, Hervé. It's your turn,' yelled Henri.

Hervé put the ball down ready and, 'One, two, three,' he kicked.

'Oh, blast!' he said, as the ball went up in the air in the wrong direction. Hélène watched it go over the playground fence.

'Hard luck, Hervé!' she said.

'Where is the ball?' Hervé asked, worried.

'It's in the road,' Henri said, and Hélène, who was looking in that direction, added,

'Oh no! Look, there's a dog.'

> Arrête, Bouboul.
> Qu'est-ce qu'il y a?
> Méchant Bouboul!

The dog saw the ball come over the fence and he wanted to get it. His owner, the old lady, hadn't noticed. She didn't understand why he was pulling on the lead.

'Stop it, Bouboul. What's the matter? Naughty Bouboul!' she cried.

Bouboul picked up the ball and started to run.

By this time the three H's had rushed up.

   'Look at the dog,' Henri said.

   'Look at its mouth,' Hervé shouted. And Hélène echoed,

   'And your ball is in its mouth.'

The dog was racing across the road when the old lady shouted,

   'Stop, Bouboul. It's red. It's dangerous!'

'It's green,' Hélène said as the light changed.

'Cross quickly,' shouted Hervé.

One behind the other, all chasing Bouboul, went Hélène, followed by Hervé, Henri and last of all the old lady.

'Get hold of the lead,' said Henri.

The old lady kept on scolding the dog. 'Naughty Bouboul. Stop!'

Bouboul was worn out. He sat panting on the other side of the road.
There at his feet was the flattened ball.

'What's the matter?' asked the old lady.

'Look at my ball!' said Henri, gazing in horror at his squashed ball.

'And tomorrow it's the match at school,' added Hélène.

'And Henri's playing,' said Hervé.

The three H's knew there was no way to practise without a ball.

Écoutez. Restez ici. Je reviens. Il y a une petite boutique dans le square.

'Listen,' said the old lady. 'Stay here. I'll be back. There's a little shop in the square.' And without saying more she hurried away in the direction of the square, grasping Bouboul's lead tightly.

The old lady went into the shop and started to look at the different balls.

'What colour, Madam?' the man said. 'Red? Pink? Black-and-white?'

The old lady thought for a moment, then said,

'Let's see. A big black-and-white ball, please, and a little red ball.'

She hurried back to the children.

'There. One ball for you,' she said, pushing a ball into Henri's hands. 'Play well tomorrow.'

'Oh, brilliant,' said Hervé. 'It's a football.'

'Yes,' cheered Hélène. 'It's a real one.'

Henri beamed.

'Thank you, Madam,' he said.

Next day they all went to the match. Henri took his new football and his team won. He came out with the team to show off the cup.

'Brilliant!' said Hervé, jumping up and down. 'He's won!'

'Bravo Henri,' cheered Hélène.

The old lady looked on smiling. Bouboul sat proudly with his new red ball in his mouth. Henri looked at them.

'Thank you, Bouboul,' he shouted and the whole team joined in.

Games to play

Touche ton nez   Touch your nose

How to play

1 Choose one player to be leader.
2 He or she tells the other players what to
   do in French, like this:
   'Touche ton nez.'   'Touche ta bouche.'
   'Touch your nose.'   'Touch your mouth.'
   'Touche tes yeux.'
   'Touch your eyes.'
   The players have to touch their nose, their
   mouth or some part of their body.
3 If they do the wrong thing, or move
   their hand when the leader says mon, ma,
   mes (my) or son, sa, ses (his, her, its)
   instead of ton, ta, tes (your), they are out.
4 The last one who is left wins and is
   leader next time.

'Bouboul, touche ta queue.'
'Bouboul, touch your tail.'

Who won?   Qui a gagné?
Did you?
Oui. J'ai gagné.
Yes. I've won.
Non. Il a gagné.
No. He's won.
Non. Elle a gagné.
No. She's won.

Quelle couleur?   What colour?

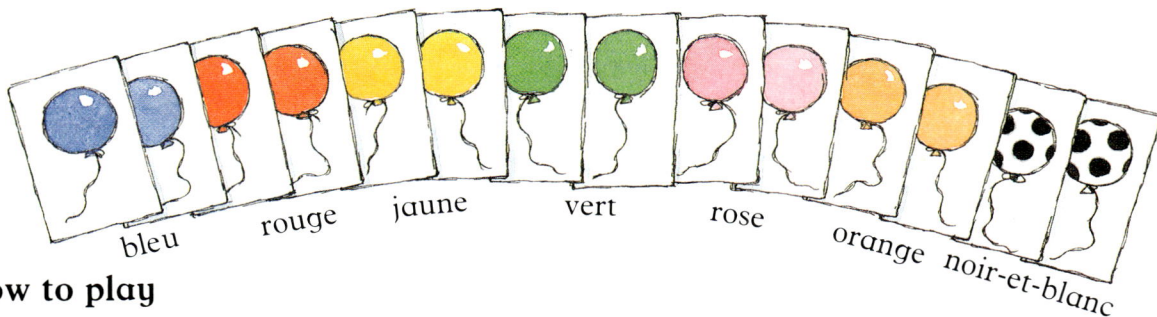

bleu   rouge   jaune   vert   rose   orange   noir-et-blanc

How to play

1 Make 2 cards like these for each colour balloon.
2 Take out one card and hide it without looking at it or showing it to anyone.
3 Deal out the remaining cards one by one to the players.
4 Each player looks at his or her cards and takes out any pair of balloons of the same colour.
5 The first player then asks the second: 'As-tu un ballon rouge?' 'Have you a red balloon?'

6 If the other player has got one, he says: 'Oui. J'en ai un.' 'Yes, I have got one,' He then gives it to the first player who makes another pair. If he hasn't got one, he says: 'Non. Je n'en ai pas.' 'No, I haven't got one.'
7 The second player then asks the third player, and so on.
8 The game continues until one player is left with one card. This player has lost.

As-tu un ballon rose?

Oui. J'en ai un.

Who lost?   Qui a perdu?

Did you?
Oui. J'ai perdu.
Yes, I've lost.
Non. Elle a perdu.
No, she's lost.
Non. Il a perdu.
No, he's lost.

19

A song to sing

Dites avec nous:
Say with us:

Chantez avec nous:
Sing with us:

l'oeil

le nez

la bouche

le cou

le ventre

le genou

le pied

En passant les Pyrénées,
Il y a de la neige,
Il y a de la neige.
En passant les Pyrénées,
Il y a de la neige. . .

Jusqu'aux pieds.

20

Jusqu'aux genoux.

Jusqu'au ventre.

Jusqu'au cou.

Jusqu'à la bouche.

Jusqu'au nez.

Jusqu'aux yeux.

Going over the Pyrénées (mountains),
There's some snow.
There's some snow up to . . .

21

Talking to each other

C'est à qui?
Whose is it?

C'est à moi.
It's mine.

Ce n'est pas à toi.
It's not yours.

Oui. J'en ai.
Yes, I have.

Non. Je n'en ai pas.
No, I haven't got one.

As-tu un ballon bleu?
Have you a blue balloon?

As-tu un ballon rose?
Have you got a pink balloon?

Qu'est-ce qu'il y a?
What's the matter?

Alors, mange du pain.
Then eat some bread.

J'ai faim.
I'm hungry.

Et j'ai soif.
And I'm thirsty.

Alors, bois de l'eau.
Then drink some water.

22

Touche son nez.
Touch its nose.

Alors, touche sa bouche.
Then touch its mouth.

Je ne peux pas.
I can't.

Non, C'est dangereux.
No, it's dangerous.

Que veut dire 'tête'?
Je ne comprends pas.
What does 'tête' mean?
I don't understand.

Regarde. C'est ma tête.
Look, this is my head.

O.K.
I've got it.

23

Rhymes and sums

$2 + 2 = 4$ Deux et deux font quatre.

Un, deux, trois,
Ma boule.
Quatre, cinq, six,
Qui roule,
Sept, huit, neuf,
Sur la pelouse,
Dix, onze, douze,
Jusqu'à Toulouse.

One, two, three,
My bowling ball.
Four, five, six,
Is rolling,
Seven, eight, nine,
On the grass,
Ten, eleven, twelve,
Up to Toulouse (a city).

A, B, C,
J'ai gagné.
O, P, Q,
J'ai perdu.

A, B, C,
I've won.
O, P, Q,
I've lost.

J'ai faim.
Mange ta main.
Garde l'autre
Pour demain.
Et ta tête
Pour les jours de fête.

I'm hungry.
Eat your hand.
Keep the other
For tomorrow.
and your head
For the special holidays.

$5 + 5 = 10$ Cinq et cinq font dix. $4 + 4 = 8$ Quatre et quatre font huit.

Finger puppets

1 Trace the faces on to a piece of paper.
2 Colour the faces in.
3 Stick double-sided sticky tape on the back of the paper.
4 Cut out the faces.
5 Peel the backing off the tape and stick the faces on your fingers.
6 Make your puppets talk in French, using the words on pages 22/23.

Saying it right

Whose croissant is it?

C'est mon croissant.

It's my croissant.

C'est ton croissant.

It's your croissant.

C'est son croissant.

It's his croissant.

Whose ice-cream is it?

C'est ma glace.

It's my ice-cream.

C'est ta glace.

It's your ice-cream.

C'est sa glace.

It's his ice-cream.

In French, words for things and people are either:

Masculine:	*mon croissant*	*ton croissant*	*son croissant*	*un croissant*	*le croissant*
or Feminine:	*ma glace*	*ta glace*	*sa glace*	*une glace*	*la glace*

They have got to be one or the other and there are some surprises.

Look at:
  une balle
  a small ball

  un ballon
  a balloon/ball

  une balle de tennis
  a tennis ball

  un ballon de foot
  a football

  une boule
  a bowl

  une boule de neige
  a snowball

What colour?

Quelle couleur?

C'est mon ballon rouge.

C'est mon ballon jaune.

C'est mon ballon vert.

C'est mon ballon bleu-et-rose.

C'est mon ballon blanc-et-noir.

C'est ma balle rouge.

C'est ma balle jaune.

C'est ma balle verte.

C'est ma balle bleue-et-rose.

C'est ma balle blanche-et-noire.

How big is it?

C'est un grand ballon.
It's a big balloon.

C'est une grande glace.
It's a big ice-cream.

C'est un petit ballon.
It's a little balloon.

C'est une petite glace.
It's a little ice-cream.

I can Speak French

What do these mean?
Check on the pages shown.

J'ai faim. 22

Pas de chance! 8

Quelle couleur? 15

Écoutez! 14

Elle a gagné. 18

C'est à qui? 22

Voilà. 16

Il y a de la neige. 20

Je ne peux pas. 23

C'est dans la rue. 9

Non. Je n'en ai pas. 19

Joue avec moi. 4

S'il vous plaît. 15

C'est à moi. 7

C'est dangereux! 11

Il y a une petite boutique. 14

D'accord. 4

Qu'est-ce qu'il y a? 13

Vas-y! 6

Can you find all these words in the pictures? Oui ou non?

Did you know all the words?
Could you find all the names?
If you like speaking French,
make yourself a badge
that says so.

1 Trace the badge on thin paper.
2 Put your tracing paper on top
   of a sticky label and press
   through the shape and letters.
3 Colour the badge and cut it out.
   Wear it with pride.

J' ❤ aime le français

Bravo!

Bien!

Très bien!

J'aime le français!

Index and words to remember

Aa

l'alimentation	food shop
l'alphabet	the alphabet

Bb

une balle	a little ball 5
un ballon	a balloon or big ball 15
blanc	white 15
bleu	blue 19
un bonnet à pompon	a bobble hat
un bonnet de ski	a ski hat
une bouche	a mouth 11
un boulanger	a baker 5
une boule	a bowling ball 24
une boutique	a small shop 14
un bureau de poste	a post office

Cc

une chanson	a song
un chien	a dog 9
cinq	five 24
un coiffeur	a hairdresser
un cou	a neck 20
une coupe	a cup

Dd

une dame	a lady
deux	two 24
dix	ten 24
douze	twelve 24

Ee

l'eau	water 22
une école	a school 13
une église	a church

Ff

un feu rouge	a red traffic light
les feux	traffic lights
une fille	a girl

Gg

un garçon	a boy
un genou	a knee 20
grand	big/large 15

Hh

un homme	a man
huit	eight 24

Ii

une invitation	an invitation

Jj

un jour de fête	a holiday 24
un journal	a newspaper
jaune	yellow 19
un jeu	a game

Kk

un kilomètre	a kilometre

Ll
une laisse	a lead
une librairie	a bookshop 11
un lion	a lion
un livre	a book

Mm
marron	brown
une main	a hand 24
un match	a match 13
un match de football	a football match

Nn
la neige	snow 20
un nez	a nose 18
noir	black 15

Oo
un oeil	an eye 20
onze	eleven 24
orange	orange 19

Pp
le pain	bread
une papeterie	a stationery shop
un passage clouté	a traffic crossing
une pelouse	a grass lawn 24
petit	little/small 14
une pharmacie	a chemist's shop 11
un pied	a foot 20

Qq
quatre	four 24
une question	a question
une queue	a tail 18

Rr
rouge	red 11
une rue	a road/a street 9

Ss
un sandwich	a sandwich
sept	seven 24
six	six 24
un square	a square 14

Tt
une tête	a head 23
une toilette	a toilet
trois	three 24
un trottoir	a pavement

Uu
un	one 24

Vv
un ventre	a stomach 20
une voiture	a car

Yy
les yeux	eyes 18

Making the best of this book

Children learn a language (including their own) by first hearing and understanding it, and then imitating it. To begin with, they pick up words and phrases – blocks of language – that they can use in everyday situations. At first their pronunciation and grammar may not be correct, but there's no need to 'get it right'. Children naturally change their speech, bit by bit, to get it closer to what they hear. That's how this book works.

Everyone enjoys success. Praise encourages children to learn more and more. Here are some useful words: *Bien! Très bien! Bravo!* If you can't speak French, it is better not to try to read the French because you may pronounce it wrong. Get the cassette or ask someone who knows French to read the book out loud for you. All the family can share in learning French at the same time.

Below we suggest ways that may help you use this book and get the best out of it. You will probably find many others, too.

Steps to success

1 Get someone to read the story out loud in English. Then listen to the story on the cassette – or ask someone who speaks French to read it. Look at the pictures and listen carefully to the French.
   Listen to the ABC song on the cassette and point to the letters on pages 30/31.

2 Listen to the story again, following in the book and repeating the French words.
   Sing the ABC song again and play the game on page 18.

3 Listen to the story again. By now you can probably join in.
   Sing the ABC song again and play the game on page 19.

4 Say the numbers and listen to the marching song on the cassette. Look at the pictures on pages 20/21. You can march up and down like the three H's as you sing.

5 Look at the pictures on pages 22/23 and listen to what all the characters say on the cassette.

6 Listen to the rhymes and number chants on the cassette. Repeat them and follow the words on page 24. Can you remember the rhymes?

7 Make the puppets on page 25. Listen to the story again as you do so. Then make the puppets act. They can say the words on pages 22/23. They can sing the song on pages 20/21 and say the rhymes on page 24.

8 Make a puppet of the old lady and the shopkeeper and act out the whole story. Get your friends to help you.

9 Get the puppets to play the games on pages 18/19. Sing the marching song with them.

10 See if you can 'say it right' with your puppets or with your friends (pages 26/27).

11 Did you find all the phrases and words on page 28? Do you know what they mean? Can you say them right?

12 Now you are speaking French. *Bravo! Bien! Très bien!* Make yourself a badge, and show off your French to your friends!